HEROSTORIES

ÍSLAND.

HEROSTORIES
HETJUSÖGUR

Kristín Svava Tómasdóttir

Translated from the Icelandic by K.B. Thors

PHONEME
MEDIA

DEEP
VELLUM

DALLAS, TEXAS

Phoneme Media, an imprint of Deep Vellum
3000 Commerce St., Dallas, Texas 75226
deepvellum.org · @deepvellum

Deep Vellum Publishing
3000 Commerce St., Dallas, Texas 75226
deepvellum.org · @deepvellum

Deep Vellum is a 501c3 nonprofit literary arts organization
founded in 2013 with the mission to bring
the world into conversation through literature.

FIRST PRINTING

Publication of this book was helped in part by funding from the
Alberta Foundation for the Arts.

ISBN: 978-1-64605-228-8 (paperback)
ISBN: 978-1-64605-254-7 (eBook)

LIBRARY OF CONGRESS CONTROL NUMBER: 2022951820

Cover design by Emily Lee
Interior layout & typesetting by KGT

PRINTED IN THE UNITED STATES OF AMERICA

The poems in this book are composed entirely of text from Íslenskar ljósmæður I—III, Icelandic Midwives I—III, an account of 100 Icelandic midwives who worked around the island through the nineteenth and early twentieth centuries. Compiled and published by Rev. Sveinn Víkingur between 1962 & 1964, Icelandic Midwives *has three general kinds of entries: those written by the midwives themselves, those written by others who knew or knew of them, and those written by the priests collecting the material.*

Í minningu systur minnar, Ástríðar Tómasdóttur

In memory of my sister, Ástríður Tómasdóttir

Þýðingin er tileinkuð Ellen Nínu Ingolfsson

Translation dedicated to Ellen Nína Ingolfsson

CONTENTS

HEROSTORIES

Okkur órar sjaldnast fyrir því
hversu mikils við höfum
                    fyrir hirðuleysi okkar
farið á mis

                    fyrr en á gröfum hinna dauðu

We seldom imagine
how much we have
                    for our carelessness
mislaid

                    until we arrive at the graves of the dead

græni bletturinn í urðinni
undir hamrinum háa
geymir ekki aðeins sögu hins bjartsýna framtaks

hann geymir sögu hinnar hljóðu og örðugu baráttu
hann er vættur tárum mikilla harma
og þungrar sorgar

þaðan hafa heitar bænir stigið í himininn
í beiskri kvöl
og þungri neyð

the green spot on the scree
under the high cliff face
holds not only history of optimistic enterprise

it holds story of silent and difficult struggle
it is wet with tears of great lament
and heavy sorrow

from there fervent prayers have risen to heaven
in bitter agony
and heavy distress

misskilningur sem menn stundum
í hugsunarleysi
hafa um gamla tímann

af honum sé ekkert hægt að læra
hann sé eins og

  ranglega orðuð setning
  sem strika þurfi yfir

    sem vendilegast

misunderstandings that people sometimes
in thoughtlessness
have about the old times

that nothing can be learned from them
they are like

      a wrongly worded sentence
      that must be struck out

            most carefully

fennir í flestra spor
sagnir máðar
af spjöldum minninganna

þessar línur aðeins tilraun
til að bjarga fáeinum
merkiskonum
úr fönninni

snow in most tracks
stories obscured
from pagebound memory

these lines only attempt
to save a few
remarkable women
from the drifts

mæður lífs og ljóss

báru ljós í bæina
blessuðu yfir vöggu barnanna
klæddu sig úr fötunum
til að gefa konunum

göfug þjónusta við lífið
heilög þjónusta við lífið og höfund þess

um nafnlausa minningu þeirra leikur fögur birta

mothers of life and light

brought light into houses
blessings over children's cradles
took clothes off their backs
to give the women

noble service to life
sacred service to life and its author

around their nameless memory plays a beautiful brightness

einhvers staðar í fórum sínum átti hún ofurlítinn kassa
fullan af smámiðum
og vísa eða kvæðisbrot krotað með blýanti á hvern þeirra

þessar hendingar höfðu leitað framrásar
líkt og lindin undan berginu
eða stráið úr moldinni

seinna
þegar tóm gafst til
raðaði hún sumu af þessu saman í kvæði

somewhere in her possession she had a tiny box
full of smallpaperslips
and verses or poemscrap scrawled in pencil on each one

these lines sought to flow forth
like the spring under rock
or straw through soil

later
when time allowed
she arranged some of these together in a poem

~

Hún var snemma öll og óskipt þar
sem nýr einstaklingur lét á sér bæra
gældi við allt sem var fagurt og veikburða
blómin og lömbin og ungana á vorin
kálfana og folöldin

From an early age she was always there
wherever a new person came into being
caressed all that was beautiful and delicate
the flowers and the lambs and chicks in spring
the calves and foals

fyrir

    barnaskap og forvitni

        forvitni og hégómaskap

hendingu eða tilviljun   hátíðlegt heit

        minningu um gamlan draum

dulin öfl   forlög

        forlög

vísbendingu í draumi   loforð álfkonunnar

        vitjanir látinna manna

dulda kennd   innri köllun

        þrá

af

    einhverri

        ómótstæðilegri

           þrá

out of

       childishness and curiosity

         curiosity and vanity

coincidence or chance   a solemn vow

      a memory of an old dream

mysterious forces   fate

       fate

directions in a dream   an elfwoman's promise

       visits from dead folk

secret sense   inner calling

      yearning

through

     some

      irresistible

        yearning

hún var fædd til þess
að líkna og hjúkra
það var henni í eðlið borið
hjúkrunar- og lækniseðlið
ættarfylgja

                    mann fram af manni

she was born for this
to treat and nurse
it was in her nature
the nursing and healing
hereditary

                    from person to person

hneigð
hneigð til líknar
hneigð til líknarstarfa
hneigð til lækninga og líknarstarfa
hneigð til að hjúkra hjúkra sjúkum
hneigð til að hjálpa hjálpa og líkna
hneigð til að binda um sárin

keen
keen on caring
keen on charity
keen on healing and relief
keen to nurse nurse the sick
keen to help help and comfort
keen on binding the wound

meðfædd líknarlund
meðfædd löngun
til að líkna og hjúkra sjúkum
til að vera hjá fæðandi dýrum

löngun
löngun til að læra
löngun til aukins víðsýnis
löngun til að öðlast tilbreytingu
löngun til að hleypa heimdraganum
löngun til að verða eitthvað meira en eldabuska

knúði sífellt á

inborn benevolence
inborn longing
to comfort and nurse the sick
to be there for birthing animals

longing
longing to learn
longing for broader horizons
longing for a change of scenery
longing to leave home
longing to be something more than a cook

compelled ever on

þrá
þrá til að læra
þrá til að menntast
þrá til að litast um í heiminum
þrá til að kynnast einhverju öðru meiru
þrá til

að verða

yearning
yearning to learn
yearning to study
yearning to look around the world
yearning to get to know something else something more
yearning

to become

stóð hugur hennar fremur til náms en búsýslu

ef hún hefði verið fædd á þessari öld
hefði hún numið læknisfræði

bara að ég hefði orðið drengur

her mind was on study rather than housework

if she had been born in this century
she would have studied medicine

if only I had been a boy

lærdómsbrölt
helber hégómi

slíkt ódæði þótti þá
að stúlkur lærðu að skrifa!

þú ert ekki orðin hreppstjóri ennþá!

allan vilja varð að bæla niður
allt varð að gerast í felum

learningnonsense
sheer vanity

such outrageous thoughts back then
girls learning to write!

you're not sheriff yet!

all will had to be suppressed
everything had to happen in hiding

las allar bækur sem hún náði í
las allar bækur sem hún náði í

                                    drakk í sig

read all the books she could find
read all the books she could find

absorbed

pappírssneplar

    reyttir saman pappírssneplar

gamlir reikningar

           fjaðurpenni fjaðurpenni
                úr álftafjaðrarlegg

    pennastöng
    úr klofinni spýtu

tólg og flot
brætt í kerti

        blekið sót
        úr eldhúsinu

        blekið sortulögur
           kálfsblóð

papersnippets

      pulled together papersnippets

old accounts

             featherpen featherpen
                of swanfeather

    penstem
    of split stick

tallow and fat
melted into candle

            the ink soot
            from the kitchen

            the ink boiledheather
               calf's blood

~

Hún unni börnunum
fuglunum fleygu
og ferfættum dýrum

hug hennar áttu
hin björtu sund

sálarlíf hennar slungið sterkum
en ólíkum og andstæðum þáttum
tilfinningar hennar svo heitar
að hún var svo að segja öll á valdi þeirra

She loved the children
fledgling birds
and fourfooted animals

her soul belonged
to the bright broad channels

her nature wove strong
but different and opposing elements
so heated were her feelings
that she was so to speak totally at their will

í senn sterk og höfðingleg
og svo mild og hlý

mátti ekkert aumt sjá
    ekkert aumt sjá
    ekkert aumt sjá
án þess að reyna úr að bæta

líknsöm var hún við aumingja
greiðug við fátæka
mjúkhent við veika
nærgætin við sjúka
hjálpsöm við þá sem áttu bágt

trú hennar á það góða í lífinu máttug og sterk
                furðulega máttug og sterk

lotningin djúp
fyrir dásemdum lífsins

at once strong and dignified
and so mild and warm

could not see woe
        not see woe
        not see woe
without trying for better

she was gracious with the wretched
open with the poor
softhanded with the weak
caring with the sick
helpful with those in need

her belief in the good in life powerful and strong
                        amazingly powerful and strong

deep reverence
for the wonders of life

hugur hennar stóð hærra en almennt gerðist
engin var hún volæðis- eða kenjasál

skemmti sér við lestur bóka og ritgjörða
sem ekki voru við alþýðuhæfi

átti hið innra í sjálfri sér
bjartan heim drauma og ljóða

kunni að umgangast háa sem lága
kunni að taka á móti gestum
kunni að hlýða á mál manna
kunni að segja frá

hagmælt var hún en hélt því lítið á lofti
skáldmælt nokkuð þótt hún flíkaði því lítt
dável hagmælt en flíkaði ekki þeirri gáfu
gat komið saman vísu en hélt því ekki á lofti

frábitin því
að segja af sér afrekasögur

her mind ranged higher than common happenings
no miser- or mutable soul was she

enjoyed herself reading books and essays
not suited to popular taste

had within herself
a bright world of dreams and poems

knew how to get along with high and low
knew how to receive guests
knew how to heed folks' talk
knew how to tell a story

she was poetically inclined but kept that close to her chest
skaldtongued though she flaunted it little
speechdeft indeed but did not flaunt those gifts
could compose on the spot but held verse close to her chest

far be it from her
to speak of her achievements

hún var eigi óskyggn á hina huldu vegi sálarlífsins
sjaldnast varbúin stærri tíðindum

óraði fyrir mörgu
sá gegnum veggi og holt og hæðir
                           sá lengra

fór svo um margt sem hana grunaði

she was not unseeing of the hidden ways of the soul
seldom surprised by major tidings

sensed many things
saw through walls and woods and hills

                                    saw further

many things went as she expected

handtak hennar var hlýtt
og loforð hennar brugðust aldrei

glaðværð hennar glæddi
von og trú í veikum huga
stráði geislum á veg samferðamanna
lyfti henni yfir öldur mótlætis og harma

hún hafði stundum orð á því í viðtali
hvað það væri gaman að lifa

her handshake was warm
and her promise never failed

her cheerfulness kindled
hope and faith in the minds of the sick
scattered rays on the road for fellow travelers
lifted her over waves of adversity and sorrow

she sometimes mentioned in conversation
how great it is to be alive

virt og elskuð
elskuð og virt
elskuð og virt af öllum

að þóknast henni gerði hvern mann meiri

svipurinn einbeittur og þróttmikill
svipurinn göfugur og skýr
drottningarsvipur

respected and loved
loved and respected
loved and respected by all

to please her made any man proud

her expression focused and powerful
her expression noble and clear
a queen's expression

svipur hennar bjartur og hreinn
svipur hennar hreinn og fagur

heimilishamingja
aufúsugestur

her expression bright and clean
her expression clean and beautiful

householdhappiness
a welcome guest

orðfleygt var um þrek hennar og dugnað

wordflew about her endurance and drive

trúmennsku skörungsskap gáfur og glaðlyndi hagvirkni
og gott hjarta starfshneigð og atorku víðsýni og
hugkvæmni næmi og starfshæfni gáfur atorku þrek til
líkama og sálar alúð dáð hennar til starfa samviskusemi
greind og athygli líkamsþrek þolinmæði kjark kunnáttu
og handlagni gáfur kunnáttu og handlagni fórnarlund
kjark og dugnað kærleika og umburðarlyndi fórnfýsi
og dugnað iðjusemi og atorku óvenjulega fórnfýsi og
ósérplægni dugnað og drengskap um allt óbilandi vilja
röskleika hugrekki og úrræðasemi geðprýði og léttlyndi
mannelsku og óbifandi guðstrú greind trúfestu dugnað
kærleikslund skapfestu áræði og æðruleysi orðfimi og
rökvísi kjark og áræði sparneytni og hirðusemi afköst og
þol lipurð og skilning alúð og þolinmæði smekkvísi í öllu
lífsviðhorfi skilning fórnarlund og hjálpfýsi höfðingslund
gáfur eftirtekt viljaþrek og festu dugnað og skyldurækni og
dugnað greind skapfestu og næmleika drengskap óbilandi
baráttuþrek gáfur festu og einbeitni fórnfýsi ósérhlífni
gáfur og hæfileika myndarskap ráðdeild andlegt fjör
hrífandi sæmd og prýði fórnfýsi og hæfileika fórnarlund
góðvild gáfur kjark dugnað áræði snerpu líkamlegt þrek
brennandi áhuga áræði kjark dugnað þrek myndarbrag

constancy leadership intelligence and cheer efficiency and a good heart inclination to work and energy perspective and ingenuity discernment and vocational adeptness intelligence drive stamina of body and soul tenderness devotion to her work conscientiousness astuteness and attention bodilyendurance patience courage adeptness and handiness intelligence skills and handiness selfsacrifice courage and diligence charity and forbearance sacrifice and diligence industriousness and energy unusual sacrifice and unselfishness diligence and honor through everything unwavering will briskness bravery and resourcefulness gentility and lightheartedness humanity and unshakeable faith astuteness fidelity diligence and charity backbone daring and serenity eloquence and logic courage and daring economy and neatness performance perseverance and agility understanding care and patience taste in every attitude understanding selfsacrifice and helpfulness nobility intelligence and observation willpower and firmness diligence and duty diligence astuteness backbone and sensitivity honor and unwavering fight intelligence firmness and focus sacrifice unshirking

kappgirni stjórnsemi hagsýni myndarbrag reglusemi
vinnugleði alúð og kostgæfni vandvirkni og samviskusemi
hjálpfýsi og hjartahlýju mannkosti og starfshæfni
alúð og samviskusemi alúð og samviskusemi þolgæði
stillingu kunnáttu ósérplægni dugnað einbeitni dugnað
skyldurækni ráðdeild örlæti hjálpfýsi stjórnsemi gestrisni
andlegt og líkamlegt atgervi trygglyndi og vinfestu alúð
öryggi fórnfýsi dugnað og skyldurækni skyldurækni
og skilyrðislausa rausn fórnfúst hugarfar nærfærni
óbilandi kjark og þrek og dugnað þrek áhuga og dugnað
lífsgleði kjark og nákvæmni öryggi festu skörungsskap
stjórnsemi kjark og rausn áræði öryggi og dugnað

selflessness intelligence and talent prowess thrift and spiritual zest captivating honor and manners sacrifice and talent selfsacrifice goodwill intelligence and courage diligence daring agility physical stamina burning interest daring courage diligence and stamina a shining example zeal authority prudence a shining example of orderliness workjoy care and exactitude precision and conscientiousness helpfulness and warmheartedness virtues and skills care and conscientiousness care and conscientiousness perseverance equanimity adeptness and unselfishness diligence focus and diligence duty thrift generosity helpfulness authority and hospitality spiritual and physical abilities fealty and friendship care certitude sacrifice diligence and duty duty and unconditional openhandedness a selfless mindset tact and unwavering courage stamina diligence endurance and zeal diligence lifejoy courage and precision certitude firmness leadership and authority courage generosity daring certitude and diligence

góð kona
sæmdarkona
sæmdar- og gæfukona
mikilhæf kona
atgerviskona
annáluð gæðakona
kjarnakona
merkiskona
ljóselsk fróðleikskona
starfskona
tápkona mikil
táp- og atorkukona
tilfinningakona
þrekkona mikil
þrekkona til líkama og sálar

        engin hversdagskona
        engin miðlungskona

good woman
woman of honor
woman of honor and fortune
great woman
capable woman
renowned woman of virtue
superwoman
remarkablewoman
lightloving woman of knowledge
workingwoman
woman of great vigor
vim- and vigorwoman
woman of deep emotion
woman of great endurance
woman of endurance body and soul

        no everydaywoman
        no middlingwoman

þannig var kona þessi

tign og göfgi lýsti af henni
hvar sem hún fór

þá var hún stærst
þegar mest reyndi á

thus was this woman

command and nobility announced her
wherever she went

she was greatest
when most tested

Hún var fædd til þess
að hjálpa og hughreysta
hjálpa og mýkja sár annarra
draga úr þrautum og þjáningum

hún fór af sjálfsdáðum til að hugga og styrkja

boðin og búin að hjúkra og líkna
öllum þeim
        sem stundu undir
                þungum sjúkdómskrossi

She was born for this
to help and console
help and soothe the sores of others
lighten pain and suffering

she went proffering herself to comfort and strengthen

ready and willing to nurse and care for
all those
          who sighed under
                    the heavy cross of illness

gekk um líknandi
kom fram líknandi
leggjandi smyrsl á sárin

miðlandi brauði frá sínu fátæka heimili
miðlandi af fátækt sinni
miðlandi af hlýju hjarta síns

þótti sjúkum góð nærvera hennar
og vesalingar leituðu skjóls hjá henni
til hennar var auðsótt öllum nauðleitarmönnum
var sem hinir sjúku fyndu kraft og líkn
við návist hennar

went about palliating
appeared applying palliating
salve on the wounds

sharing bread from her humble home
sharing from her own poverty
sharing from the warmth of her heart

the sick deemed good her nearness
and the hapless sought shelter with her
she was readily available to all the needy
as if the sick found power and succor
in her presence

til hennar var leitað leitað úr sveitum vitjað til sjúkra
vitjað ef slys bar að höndum sjúkdóma bar að höndum
og hjúkrunar þurfti með var til hennar leitað var hennar
vitjað var hennar vitjað er sjúkdóma og slys bar að
höndum var hennar leitað til sjúklinga var hennar vitjað
vitjað til sjúkra vitjað til veikra kölluð til sjúkra og þeirra
sem urðu fyrir meiðslum eða slysum var til hennar leitað
leitað til hennar leitað jafnan leitað iðulega er veikindi eða
slys bar að höndum vitjað ef einhver meiddi sig

á erfiðum stundum
ef eitthvað gekk að
raunir steðjuðu að heimilunum
var hennar vitjað til að hugga og styrkja
                        líkna og rétta hjálparhönd
sótt til að vera yfir veiku og deyjandi
                        deyjandi fólki

og hughreysta það
og hughreysta þá sem höfðu orðið fyrir hörmum

she was sought sought after across the countryside called for
the sick called on when an accident happened sickness hap-
pened and nursing was needed she was sought she was called
on she was called when sickness and accident happened she
was sought by the afflicted she was called called for the sick
called for the weak called on by the sick and those who had
injuries and accidents she was sought sought for she was al-
ways sought for sought for often sought out when weakness
or accident struck called upon if anyone hurt themselves

in difficult times
when something went wrong
trials befell households
she was called on to comfort and strengthen
                              care for and lend a helpinghand
fetched to watch over sick and dying
                                      dying people

and comfort them
and comfort those suffering tragedy

læknir að eðlisfari

önnur hönd héraðslæknisins

í senn ljósmóðir og læknir

ljósmóðir og læknir

í senn ljósmóðir og læknir

læknir sveitarinnar

læknir

í senn ljósmóðir og læknir þessara sveita

a physician by nature

      the other hand of the district doctor

            at once a midwife and healer

midwife and healer

            at once midwife and healer

                the county physician

   doctor

            at once midwife and physician in this country

stakk á kýlum

gerði að sárum

gerði að sárum

hreinsaði   batt um

og græddi

lanced boils

tended wounds

tended wounds

        cleaned   dressed

            and did well

hendur

gæddar furðulegum mætti til að lina þjáningar
það dró úr þrautum verkir linuðust

mjúkar og mildar
        móður og barni
                sem hún lyfti til ljóss þessa heims

hands

endowed with a strange power to ease suffering
draw out pain relieve aches

soft and mild
      mother and child
            whom she lifted to the light of this world

sterku en þó mildu og mjúku
mjúku líknarhendur
mjúku kærleikshendur
líknarhendur ljósmóðurhendur
læknis- og líknarhendur líknarhendur
læknishendur mjúku hendur læknishendur
líknarhendur ljósmóðurhendur læknishendur
ljósmóðurhendur líknarhendur
mjúkar mjúkar mjúkar læknandi hendur
smáar mjúkar og fallega lagaðar

                                ljósmóðurhendur

strong but still soft and mild
soft caring hands
soft loving hands
caringhands midwifehands
curing- and caringhands caringhands
curinghands soft hands curinghands
caringhands midwifehands curinghands
midwifehands caringhands
soft soft soft curing hands
small soft and beautifully shaped

                lightmotherhands

                midwifehands

þótt illa horfði
þrátt fyrir margs konar örðugleika
                    og mikið erfiði
aðstæður allar ófullkomnar
hreinlæti minna en skyldi
þótt óálitlega horfði
þótt illa á horfðist
þótt tæpt stæði

                    dó engin kona
                    aldrei varð neitt að
                    dó aldrei kona
                    ekki nein kona
                    ekki nokkur sængurkona
                    engin kona lést
                    engin kona lést í höndum hennar
                    engin kona dó
                    og læknis aldrei leitað
                            (enda lítið um lækna)
                    aldrei henti hana óhapp
                    aldrei dó kona

though things looked bad
despite many kinds of difficulty
                        and much toil
conditions all imperfect
hygiene less than ideal
though it did not look promising
though the worst was expected
though there were close calls

              no woman died
              nothing ever went wrong
              women never died
              not one woman
              not a single woman in labor
              no woman perished
              no woman passed away in her hands
              no woman died
              and doctors never sought
                    (doctors were few anyway)
              never did she have a mishap
              women never died

nema ein sængurkona
aðeins ein kona
eitt barn óskírt
aðeins þrjú börn nýfædd
tvö eða þrjú andvana
aðeins í eitt skipti
           urðu endalokin dapurleg

except for one woman in childbed
only one woman
one unbaptized child
only three newborn babies
two or three stillborn
only one time
                    was the ending sad

varla þótti einleikið
undravert og stundum
                ganga kraftaverki næst

mun slíkt fátítt
ef ekki einstætt

hardly seemed natural
wondrous and sometimes
                    approaching the realm of miracle

such a thing is rare
if not unique

hamingja og styrkur fylgdi handtökum hennar
handleiðsla Guðs brást henni ekki
með Guðs hjálp bjargaðist allt

Guð var með henni
gæfa fylgdi henni

það var eins og dauðinn hopaði frá dyrum
hvar sem hún kom

happiness and strength followed her handiwork
God's guidance did not fail her
with God's help all was saved

God was with her
good fortune followed her

it was as if death fell back out the door
wherever she went

~

Hvar er styrks að leita
ef ekki í bæninni?

hún treysti Guði
bað höfund lífsins
að standa sér við hlið

fór aldrei bænarlaus að heiman

Where to seek strength
if not in prayer?

she trusted God
bid the author of life
to stand by her side

never went prayerless away from home

bað himnaföðurinn um hjálp og styrk
bað hann ásjár í öllum vanda
treysti höfundi lífs og ljóss
treysti Guði
treysti Guði er gerir allt vel
treysti í hverri raun
trúði staðfastlega
trúði á handleiðslu Drottins náð Guðs og bænheyrslu
handleiðslu kærleika og miskunn hjálp og almætti
hjálp og handleiðslu handleiðslu forsjón og kærleika

asked the heavenlyfather for help and strength
asked his protection through any trouble
trusted the author of life and light
trusted God
trusted God who does everything well
trusted through every ordeal
believed steadfastly
believed in the Lord's guidance God's grace and prayers heard
guidance love and mercy help and almighty
help and guidance guidance providence and love

bað hann um að vera með sér í verki
bað um að allt mætti fara vel
um kraft til handa konunni
um ljós sjálfri sér til handa
aldrei hvarf bænin úr huga hennar
ljósgjafi trúarinnar
máttur þess ósýnilega
óhagganleg trú
bjargföst vissa
örugg björt og sterk

birta Guðs var í sál hennar

asked him to be with her in her work
asked that all may go well
for strength for the woman
for light for herself
the prayer never left her mind
lightgiving faith
this invisible power
unshakable faith
rocksolid certainty
sure bright and strong

God's light was in her soul

og ljós ljómaði í vitundinni
og óttinn hvarf
og hún gekk örugg og fumlaust að verki

undursamlegur kraftur
                ósýnilegar hendur
                                dásamleg birta

hinn algóði og alvísi skapari ljóss og lífs
gaf að allt fór vel
gaf að allt fór vel

and light shone in her mind
and fear disappeared
and she went sure and straight to work

marvelous power
                    invisible hands
                                        wonderful brightness

the allgood and allknowing creator of light and life
granted that all went well
granted that all went well

Þá lýstu ekki rafmagnsljós úr gluggum
þá reyndi meira á líkamsþrek og þol
þá var margt öðruvísi en nú er

nú þarf ekki annað en styðja á hnapp
þá er komið ljós í öllum áttum
og sest að matborði
í hlýrri stofu
ekið á bíl á sléttum vegum
yfir brúaðar ár
landshorna í milli

ungt fólk
sem veltir sér í auraflóði nútímans
mun naumast trúa því að þetta sé satt

erfiðið
í ljósleysi aldanna

Then there was no electric light from the windows
then strength and stamina mattered more
then much was different than it now is

now all you have to do is press a button
then light comes from all directions
sitting down at the dinner table
in a warm living room
driving a car on smooth roads
over bridged rivers
from one corner of the country to the other

young people
swimming in pools of modern coin
will hardly believe this to be true

the difficulty
the darkness of centuries

byggðin að vísu fögur
í sólskini og sumardýrð

fagur flóinn
er sólin glitrar sund og eyjar

og tignarleg traustu fjöllin
standa þéttum fótum er stormar æða

en allir vita að í mestu manndrápsbyljunum
er konum gjarnast að taka léttasóttina

og helst að næturlagi

the homestead certainly beautiful
in sunshine and summer glory

beautiful the bay
as the sun glitters on streams and islands

and majestic solid mountains
stand firmfooted as storms rage

but everyone knows women like to go into labour
during the deadliest blizzards

and usually at night

vakna af værum blundi
búast til ferðar um langan veg
skilja við börnin grátandi og veik
til að hjálpa og bjarga börnum annarra
sárþreytt sárlasin illa fyrir kölluð
sjálf ófrísk
sjálf að því komin að ala barn
oft ekki fyrr komin heim frá einni sængurkonu
        en hennar var vitjað til þeirrar næstu

waking from sound sleep
preparing for a long trek
parting with children crying and sick
to help and save the children of others
very tired very sick in bad shape
herself pregnant
herself about to give birth to a child
often barely home from one labouringwoman
                    before she was called to the next

fór ekki á mis við andstreymi og raunir
fór ekki varhluta af þungbærri reynslu
og sárum hörmum
andstreymi óblíðum kjörum
og þungum raunum

lífið krafðist svo mikils af henni
undravert
að kraftar hennar skyldu ekki bila

did not escape calamity and trial
was not spared harrowing experience
or piercing affliction
calamity brutal conditions
and heavy tribulation

life demanded so much of her
amazing
that her strength should not falter

óttast
harma

        þá var ekkert nema sársaukinn

þola
undir þögninni

        það eru svo margir sem missa

fear
grief

        then there was nothing but pain

suffering
under silence

        there are so many in mourning

leggja af stað út í svarta vetrarnóttina
út í iðulausa stórhríð
út í hríðina og myrkrið

bæirnir á kafi
þessar litlu þústir
dökku þústir
heimkynni lífsins
þar sem fólk starfar
stríðir og elskar

set off into the black winternight
out into a ceaseless blizzard
out into the snowstorm and dark

the farms submerged
these little mounds
dark mounds
homes of the living
where people work
struggle and love

vegir í slæmu ásigkomulagi vatnsföll óbrúuð vegir slæmir
víða slæmir ekki brú á nokkurri á sjóleiðin skerjótt löng
og erfið í opnum árabátum torfærur óbrúaðar ár og brattar
hlíðar vegir engir né brýr á vatnsföllum strandferðir engar
fjallvegir fjallvegir lítt eða ekki varðaðir yfir sand að fara
og vötn mörg vegir ógreiðir harðir straumar í sundunum
á litlum árabátum fjallvegir erfiðir og seinfarnir engir
vegir á útkjálkum í útkjálkasveitum götuslóðar á einstaka
stað engu að treysta allar ár óbrúaðar vegir engir nema
götutroðningar mýrar og forarflóar vegir svo slæmir að
nálgaðist ófæru sjóleiðin ófær einstigi framan í háum
kambi vegur slæmur vegleysur og mýrardrög vegleysur og
mýrar engir lagðir vegir um apalhraun að fara grýtt leið og
vegurinn allt annað en góður á litlum bátum fyrir opnu hafi
lendingin erfið og ótrygg heiðar óvarðaðar illfærir vegir
hvorki vegir né brýr torfærir fjallvegir djúpir og krókóttir
götuslóðar vegleysur allar ár óbrúaðar enginn vegarspotti
víðáttumiklir eyðisandar illfærir eða ófærir sundurskornir
af stórfljótum óbrúuðum jökullinn hafnlausar strandir
hvergi örugg lending nokkurri kænu samgöngur torveldar
bæja á milli yfir vötn að fara engir lagðir vegir og engar
brýr þung og mikil jökulvötn torfærur graflækir keldur og

roads in bad shape streams unbridged bad roads bad all round no bridge over any river the sea route jagged long and difficult in open rowboats obstacles unbridged rivers and steep slopes neither roads nor bridges over streams no way along the coast mountain ways mountain ways not or barely cairned sand to cross and many rivers ways obstructed rough currents in the channels on little rowboats mountain ways hard and slowgoing no roads through remote outskirts trails here and there nothing to trust all rivers unbridged no roads save for trampled paths through swamps and muddy basins ways so bad almost impassable sea route impassable a single narrow pass along a high ridge bad roads roadless and marshy roadless and swamp no roads laid to get through jagged apal lava the way rocky and the road anything but good in little boats on the open sea the landing difficult and risky uncairned exposed heaths nasty roads neither roads nor bridges treacherous mountain ways deep and crooked trails no roads all rivers unbridged no patch of road expansive deserts nasty or impassable cut off by mighty rivers without bridges the glacier harbourless beaches with no safe landing for any skiffs complicated getting between farms going

flóð stórvötn og mýrar stórþýfðir móar torfærur ár allar
óbrúaðar engir vegir lagðir hraun ógreiðir vegir ár allar
óbrúaðar vatnsmiklar jökulár hraungjár djúpir gígir og
holur óruddir vegir vegleysur opnir árabátar vegir litlir eða
engir og engin vötn brúuð enginn lagður vegarspotti til

across water no laid roads no bridges heavy and huge glacial streams obstacles gullies bogs and floods big freshets swamps tussocky plains obstacles rivers all without bridges no roads laid lava obstructed rivers all unbridged overflowing glacial rivers lava crevices deep craters holes uncleared roads roadless open rowboats little or no roads and no bridges over waters no laid stretch of road at all

umdæmið víðlent feiknastórt og víðlent og erfitt stórt og
erfitt geysivíðlent og örðugt yfirferðar geysivíðáttumikið
og fjölmennt víðlent og mannmargt umdæmið nær ótak-
markað víðlent víðlent víðlent veðrasamt og ógreitt yfir-
ferðar erfitt stórt snjóþungt ógreitt erfitt erfitt erfitt erfitt
ógreitt erfitt yfirferðar snjóþungt snjóþungt umdæmið
stórt og örðugt yfirferðar snjóþungt víðáttumikið og erfitt

með erfiðustu umdæmum
með allra snjóþyngstu sveitum
snjóþyngsli meiri en í flestum öðrum byggðum
ólíklegt að önnur umdæmi hafi verið erfiðari
og torsóttari yfirferðar

the district vast enormous and vast and difficult big and
difficult immense and arduous to cross huge and peopled
vast and populated the district near boundless vast vast
vast weatherprone and unyielding to passage difficult large
snowladen unyielding hard hard hard hard unyielding and
hard to cross snowladen snowladen the district large and
arduous to cross snowladen expansive and difficult

among the hardest districts
among the heaviest snowfall areas
more snowfall than most other counties
other districts unlikely to have been more difficult
or tougher to cross

hvíldarlaust
á postulahestunum

þriggja stunda ferð
fimm klukkustunda ferð
tíu til tólf stunda ferð

                   ef gekk sæmilega

átta kílómetrar
tuttugu kílómetrar
tuttugu og fjórir kílómetrar
þrjátíu kílómetrar
sextíu kílómetrar

fótgangandi í einum áfanga með litlum hvíldum eða engum

without rest
on apostles' horses

three hour trip
five hour trip
ten to twelve hour trip

                    if all went well

eight kilometers
twenty kilometers
twenty-four kilometers
thirty kilometers
sixty kilometers

on foot in one go with little or no rest

viðsjáll vegur
hamrar og hengiflug
niður í grængolandi sjóinn
um stórgrýttar fjörur stórgrýtta urð
snarbrattar skriður
undir snarbrattri fjallshlíð snarbrattri hamrahlíð
undir háum sjávarhömrum um stórgrýttar fjörur
flughált á hverjum steini
ólgandi brimlöðrið
öldurnar skellandi upp í hamrana

kemur skriða úr fjallinu?

dangerous drop
cliff and precipice
down into the greendeep sea
over boulderstrewn shores boulderstrewn scree
sheer landslides
under sheer mountainside sheer cliffside
under high seacliffs on boulderstrewn shores
each stone slick with frost
surf churning
waves crashing up the cliffs

is a landslide coming down the mountain?

og áin ekki umflúin eins og stórfljót flóðmikil straumþung
stórgrýtt og ströng bólgin af frosti og kulda flóði yfir alla
bakka foráttuvöxtur vatnselgur beljandi straumur hvergi
sá í eyri eða stein drunur og skruðningar ruddist fram
bólgin af frosti og flæddi yfir allt bakkafull af krapi og ís
rann ofan á ísnum valt fram kolmórauð með jakaburði
beljaði fram hlaupin upp í frosti og byl hlaupin upp í frost-
inu stórir jakar slitu af sér klakaböndin fossandi beljandi
vatnsflaumur rann ofan á ísnum ísinn að bresta hestarnir
að sökkva til botns ísinn að bresta áin að brjóta stöpul-
inn undan brúarendanum byltist fram kolmórauð og
straumhörð illfær ófær ófær ógnandi skaðræðisvatnsfall

versta vatn í allri sýslunni

and the river cannot be avoided like a majorriver great-
flood heavycurrents bigboulders and the severe swell
of frost and cold flooding all over the bank high water
levels roaring torrent sandbar or stone nowhere to be
seen thunder and shearing rushing forward the swell
of frost and flood over everything the bank full of slush
and ice sliding over the ice tumbling dirtred with ice-
chunks roaring forth the rush up in the frost and snow-
storm the rush into the frost big ice floes tearing free
from icebands gushing roaring torrential water stream-
ing over the ice the ice cracking the horses sinking to
the bottom the ice cracking the river breaking the pillar
under the end of the bridge tossing dirtred and rapids
badgoing ungoable ungoable terrifying wickedriverwater

worst water in the whole county

aldrei á ævi sinni hafði hún komið út í þvílíkt myrkur
aldrei komið út í annað eins myrkur
svo svart sem það getur verið

engin aðgreining
himins og jarðar

svarta
                svarta
                                svarta myrkur

villumyrkur í veglausri óbyggð

never in her life had she gone out in such darkness
never stepped out in such dark
so black as can be

no distinguishing
heaven and earth

black
                    black
                                    black darkness

misleadingdark in roadless wild

þæfingsófærð allar brekkur fullar af snjó ófærð sökkvandi
aurhlaup svell með sprungum og djúpum krapaelg ófærð
fannir dalurinn snjóakista illfært milli bæja ófærð ófærð
ófærð hvergi fóthvíld óhemju fönn aldrei minni en í hné
snjór yfir öllu og erfitt að rata djúpt á klaka færi illt ófærð
vegna snjóa og svellalaga melar með fáum kennileitum
ófærð ófærð brim og sjógangur ófært að ýta á flot ólendandi
með öllu ófært bæja á milli hláka og vatnavextir ófærð
hin versta ófærð hvergi örlaði fyrir vegi eða kennileitum
villugjarnt mjög sökum hríðar og myrkurs ófærð fjallið
ófært sökum hálku hjarnað og svellað hálkan svo mikil
þung erfið færð hvergi sá á dökkan díl flughálka snjór
umbrotadyngjur í brekkum og skjóli móar og móaþýfi
gangfæri afleitt hálka og krapavaðall ófærð ófærðin
afskapleg sleipt og svellað ófært yfir fjallið ófærð afskapleg
umbrota skaflar kafaófærð snjóalög mikil fönnin hvergi
grynnri en í hné og víða í mitt læri hvergi sást til vegar
fyrir fönn og myrkri fyrir hríð og myrkri öll kennileiti
á kafi í fönn botnlaus ófærð göturnar sleipar ófærð
djúpir skaflar ófærð snjór afskaplegur og ófærð dalurinn
barmafullur af snjó ekki steinn eða girðingarstaur upp
úr kafinu vond færð kafaófærð allt á kafi í fönn ófærð og

impassableslog all slopes full of snow impassable sinking mudslide ice with cracks and deep snowslush impossiblegoing impassable snowdrifts the valley a snowcoffin nastygoing between farms impassable impassable impassable no footholds supreme snowdrifts never less than kneehigh snow over everything difficult to navigate deep over ice terriblegoing impassable due to snow and ice gravel beds with few landmarks impassable impassable breakers and high rough seatides impossible to advance afloat unlandable anywhere impassable between farms thaw and flood impassable the worst impassable no glimpse of paths or landmarks anywhere the way very easily lost due to snowstorms and darkness impassable the mountain impassable due to snow crusted black ice and the slippery icy glaze such grand heavy difficult going nowhere a dark spot to be seen slippery black ice snow heaps upheaved on the slopes and in sheltered spots swamps and tussocks awful trudging black ice and wading through slush impassable extremely slick and icy impassable over the mountain impassable enormous upheaval snowdrifts impasse submerged in snow layers of snow the huge snowdrift nowhere shallower than the knee and often midthigh the

lausasnjór ófærð ófærðin óskapleg og sá ekki handaskil
fyrir myrkri og hríð og skafrenningi ófærð snjór og hálka
ófærð kyngdi niður snjó illfært að kafa djúpa og lausa
fönnina strandlengjan villugjörn og torfarin flatneskja
hvergi móaði fyrir götuslóða holt og börð grafin undir
fönnina hvergi örlaði á dökkan díl jafnóðum skóf í slóðina
þungfært að brjótast áfram brjótast gegnum fönnina

road nowhere to be seen for the snow and dark for the storm and gloom all landmarks covered in bottomless snow impassable paths slippery impassable deep snow-drifts impassable snow tremendous and impassable the valley full to the brim with snow not a stone or fencepost poking up through the snow wicked going impasse sub-merged in snow everything submerged by snowdrifts impassable and loose snow impassable the impasse hor-rible unable to see a hand in front of one's face for the dark and storm and blowing snow impassable snow and black ice impassable dumping snow nastygoing plung-ing deep and the snowdrift loose the coastline deceiv-ing and the expanse a trudge footpath nowhere to be seen hillock and plank buried under the drift nowhere a dark patch to be seen the trail ever blown over heavy-going to break onward to break through the drifts

myrkt af nóttu
úlfgrá jörð
og krapahryðjur

þyngdi í lofti og dimmdi yfir
válegt veðurhljóð í fjöllum

dark of night
wolfgray ground
and snowsquall

leaden air and dimming over
ominous weathersounds in the mountains

veðrið beint í fangið
veðrið alltaf beint í fangið
hvergi ljós að sjá á bæjum

the weather right in your face
the weather always right in your face
no light to be seen on the farms

ofviðri stórhríð snjóaði gegndarlaust sunnanhvassviðri
hláka og ofsarok af suðri mikill snjór hörkufrost snjór
mikill slæmt veður hríð og náttmyrkur stormur og frost
norðaustan stormur mikil snjókoma glórulaust veður
glórulaust veður í dynjandi rigningu norðan stormur
hörkufrost snjókoma rigning stormur blindbylur fárviðri
sem geisaði um vetrarkvöld og nótt hvassviðri og hret
frost biturt og stormur napur ofsarok hörkufrost og
fannkoma hríðarkóf stormur asahláka með hvassviðri
muggukafald stórhríðar dag eftir dag drífa vaxandi nóttin
svo dimm og drífa svo þétt drífa svo þétt að ekki sá út
úr augum dynjandi regn eins og hellt væri úr fötu ofsa
norðan rok ofsahríð skafkóf stormur aftaka norðan hríð
með mikilli fannkomu glórulaus stórhríð blind þreifandi
stórhríð norðan grenjandi stórhríð með mikilli fannkomu
með miklu frosti snjókoma mikil stórhríð stormurinn
ískrandi á frosinni þekjunni hríð stórhríð ofanhríð
norðan gaddveður frost vindur frost norðanátt með frosti
og fannfergi norðan stórviðri með miklu frosti hríðarkóf
hríðarveður hrakveður ofsaveður veðurofsinn svo mikill
blindbylur og ofsarok hús léku á reiðiskjálfi grenjandi
stórhríð stórhríð stórhríð bleytustórhríð illviðri grenjandi
stórhríð norðan hvassviðri með glórulausum hríðarsorta

rok snowstorm snowed in boundless southerly gale rok sleet and terrific windstorm from the south major snow harshfrost and snow grand awful weather snowstorm and nightmurk storms and frost northeastern storm major snowfall senseless weather senseless weather pelting rain northern storm punishing frost snowfall rain and storm blinding blizzard furious tempest that raged through winter evening and night gale force winds and wet cold snaps bitter frosts and storm tremendous biting tempest harshfrost rok and hefty snowfall blizzardbanks storm rapidthaw gale force winds heavy snowfall blizzards day after day snowbanks growing the night so dim and snowdrifts steadily growing snowdrifts steadily growing nothing to be seen out the eyes rain pelting as if poured from a bucket northern rok tremendous storm blastingsnow rok extreme northern snowstorm with major snowfall senseless blinding blizzard northern blizzard howling blizzard with major snowfall with major frost snowfall great blizzard the storm screeching against the frozen turfroof snowstorm great snowstorm blizzardbearingdown frigid northern weather frost wind frost northward with frost and severe snowstorm northern blizzards with major frost whiteoutdrifts whiteoutweather inclementweather fierce storm tremendous weather so grand blindingblizzards and terrible tempest house trembling howling hugeblizzard hugeblizzard hugeblizzard hugewetblizzard foulweather howling blizzard northern gale with senseless blizzardthickdark

stórhríð bylur ofsaveður af norðri og frost veðurofsi
ofsaveður norðanstórhríð og frost og dimmt af nóttu
norðaustan stórhríð éljagangur af norðaustri svartasta
stórhríð af norðri og frostharkan að sama skapi frost
hvassviðri og fjúkslydda og regn og húðarslagveður
stórviðri hríðar og illviðri kafþykkt loft snjókoma
mikil norðanhríð fannkoma illviðri veður hið versta
stórhríð hörkufrost hríð og dimmviðri norðandrif og
hríðarveður norðanstórviðri með mikilli snjókomu rok
og rigning vindhæðin svo mikil að gaflinn á bænum gekk
út og inn norðan rok og gekk á með byljum útsunnan
hryssingsveður með afardimmum éljum vonskuveður
myrkur og hríð ofsaveður og hörkubylur frostbitran nísti
merg og bein hörkufrost sjór úfinn hríðarbakki til hafsins
nöpur gola og frost mökkur stóð fram af hálsbrúninni
hvassviðri efra veðurútlitið ískyggilegt veðurhvinurinn
fór vaxandi hríðin lamdi stokkfreðna þekjuna blindhríð
frost og fönnin hlóðst á gluggann útsynningsél ofsarok
fannkoma og þrettán stiga frost stormur blindbylur og
fjórtán stiga frost þreifandi hríð dimmviðri og hríð miklar
hríðar grimmar og langvinnar norðan hríðar stórhríð af
norðri með veðurofsa og fannkomu snjókoma ákafleg
og lognhríð mikil hríð og náttmyrkur með dimmum éljum

blizzard snowstorm fierce storm from the north and frost tremendous gale fierce storm northernblizzard and frost and dark of night northeastern blizzard fitful squalls from the northeast the blackest blizzard from the north and similar punishing harshfrost frost gale force winds and drivingsleet and rain skinstinging weather great storm snowstorms and foulweather snowthick air immense snowfall northern snowstorm snowfall foulweather the worst weather blizzard hardfrost snowstorm and darkweather northerlywinds and snowstorms northernblizzards with immense snowfall rok and rain windspeed so great the gable on the farm shook back and forth northern rok and rattling southwestern snowstorms roughweather with extremedark squalls wickedweather darkness and snowstorm furious gale and severe storm bitter frost penetrating marrow and bone harshfrost rough seas snowstorm cloudbank from the sea biting breeze and frost snowclouds blowing over the ridge gale force winds above the weather looking sinister the windshriek growing the snowstorm beating the frozensolid roof blindingblizzard frost and the snowdrift piled against the window southwesternsquall tremendous storm snowdump and thirteen degrees below freezing storms blindingblizzards and fourteen degrees below freezing blinding snowstorm darkweather and snowstorm major snowstorms cruel and ongoing northern snowstorms grand blizzards from the north with extreme weather and snowdump snowfall terrible snowfallingstillness and great snowstorm and nightmurk with dark squalls

hesturinn trylltur
hesturinn í ánni
hesturinn í ófærðinni
hesturinn í pyttinum
hesturinn í mógröfinni
hesturinn í sandkvikunni
hesturinn í sandbleytunni
hesturinn á kafi í ánni
hesturinn á kafi í ánni
flugstraumurinn veltandi hestinum í ánni
jakarnir riðandi undir fótum hennar

lesandi faðirvorið í huganum
vildi ekki deyja svona ung

the horse wild with fear
the horse in the river
the horse in the impassable
the horse in the pit
the horse in the peat bog
the horse in quicksand
the horse in wetsand
the horse submerged in the river
the horse submerged in the river
the fleetcurrent rolling the horse in the river
the ice floe swaying under her feet

        reciting the lord's prayer in her mind
        did not want to die so young

ekki verður feigum forðað

skriður brattar og háar
hafaldan sleikjandi hátt upp í hamrana
                    líkt og gráðug tunga

gilið barmafullt af snjó

skyndilega hreyfist skaflinn
á fleygiferð niður snarbratt gilið

undir krapinu
á haf út

the fey will not be saved

scarp face steep and high
ocean breakers licking high up in the crags
                                        like a greedy tongue

the canyon full to the brim with snow

suddenly the snowdrift goes
flying down the sheer canyon slope

under seawaterslush
out to the ocean

ekki verður feigum forðað

kolmórautt
krapavatn

hafði mörgum í hel komið
og ekki búið enn

þau voru horfin
en dökkleitt rekald
flaut ofan ána

the fey will not be saved

dirtred
slushwater

many had died
and it wasn't done yet

they were gone
but dusky wreckage
floated down the river

sáu þá sem snöggvast ljós
sáu daufa glætu
sáu gegnum sortann ljóstýru í glugga
sáu daufan
      lýsandi blett
            framundan

unglingsstúlka
         með ljósker í hendi

saw then a fleeting glimpse of light
saw a faint glow
saw through the gloom a beacon in the window
saw the faint
         luminous spot
                 ahead

an adolescent girl
                 with lantern in hand

~

Aldrei var skammdegismyrkrið svo svart
frostið svo biturt
ófærðin svo mikil
hríðarkófið svo þykkt

að hún léti bilbug á sér finna
að leggja út í óveðrin

aldrei urðu vötnin henni farartálmi
aldrei brast hana kjark
aldrei dró hún úr því að lagt væri á tæpasta vaðið

Never was the shortdaydark so black
the cold so bitter
the going so heavy
the whiteout so thick

that she hesitated
to set out in unthinkable weather

never would the water bar her way
never broke her spirit
never shied away from the riskiest ford

lét ekkert aftra sér
lét ekkert aftra sér
ekki lét hún hindra sig úfinn sjó
ófær vötn illfærar skriður snjóþung fjöll
veður né vegleysur
örbirgð né andstreymi

ávallt viðbúin
ávallt tilbúin
ávallt ferðbúin

                    á skammri stund
                    örskammri stund

brá skjótt við
bjó sig af stað
út í kófið

let nothing deter her
let nothing deter her
did not let herself be hindered by rough seas
uncrossable waters nasty landslides
snowbound mountains
weather nor roadlack
want nor struggle

ever prepared
ever ready
ever travel ready

        in a quick moment
        a very quick moment

lit out at once
lived gearing up
off into the snowdrift

alltaf jafnfús til ferðar

hvernig sem viðraði
hvernig sem viðraði
hvernig sem veðri og færð var háttað
spurði aldrei um veður né færð

hikaði ekki
hikaði ekki
hikaði ekki
hikaði aldrei
hikaði aldrei
hikaði aldrei
við að leggja á fjallið

ekkert hik

engin hugsun um hættu komst að
engin hugsun um vosbúð og kulda

always equally willing to embark

whatever the weather
whatever the weather
whatever the weather and conditions
never asked about weather nor conditions

hesitated not
hesitated not
hesitated not
hesitated never
hesitated never
hesitated never
to head up the mountain

no hesitation

no thought of danger occurred
no thought of exposure and cold

af stað!
af stað undir eins í Drottins nafni!

af stað út í ofsann
horfin í sortann

snaraðist á bak og þeysti af stað
þeysti út í náttmyrkrið
yfir vegleysur og fen
út í blindvitlausar stórhríðar
út í bullandi ófærur
hvíldarlaust hélt hún móti hríðinni
fór karlvega í söðul sinn og lagði ótrauð
út í djúp og straumþung vatnsföllin
út í æðandi flauminn

onward!
onward at once in the name of the Lord!

onward out into the tempest
vanished in the whiteout

leapt on horseback and dashed off
dashed out in the nightmurk
over roadless ground and fen
out in madblind blizzards
out in rabid impasse
relentless she pressed against the storm
sat mannish astride her sidesaddle and set off unshrinking
out in deep and heavy current
out in the raging torrent

sá hún sér margan lífsháska búinn
kom alvot og klökuð úr svaðilförum
fannbarin út úr frostbyljum
en lét það ekki á sig fá

hræðsla um líf og limi komst ekki að
þegar aðrir þurftu á aðstoð hennar að halda

she saw many lifethreats awaiting her
came soaking wet and cloaked in ice from venturesome treks
snowthrashed out of frost storms
but did not let it get to her

fear for life and limb did not interfere
when others needed her help

þegar fylgdarmenn brast ratvísi
tók hún við vegsögunni
sagði til um rétta stefnu
í náttmyrkri og hríð

þættu henni fylgdarmenn seinlátir
hirti hún lítt um að bíða þeirra

teldu fylgdarmenn ekki fært
tók hún ráðin af þeim og reið út í ána

teldu karlmenn veður með öllu ófært
og engri konu fært út í slíka hríð
sagðist hún samt fara

when men accompanying her lost their bearings
she took over the navigation
declared the right course
in nightdark and storm

      if she felt her guides were lagging
      she cared little to wait for them

if escorts thought it not passable
she took charge and rode into the river

      if menfolk thought the weather
      completely impassable
      and no woman could go out in such snowstorm
      she still said go

vildi fylgdarmaður frá hverfa
sagði hún það fært
síðan sundreið hún fljótið
    og skildi þar með þeim

gengi ísbjörn á land og sögur á kreiki
að margir fleiri hefðu sést úti á ísnum
    nefndu sumir tólf
ekkert vit í að halda áfram yfir nóttina
nema í fylgd með vopnuðum mönnum
    veifaði hún hendinni
    bandaði frá sér
    var síðan horfin

the guideman would want to turn back
she would say it is doable
then swim her horse across coursing river
          and part ways with them

    a polar bear would walk ashore
    and stories go round
    about many more seen out on the ice
          some said twelve
    no sense going on overnight
    unless accompanied by armed men
          she waved her hand
          shooed them off
          then was gone

vildi halda áfram
vildi komast áfram
vildi ekki heyra annað nefnt en halda áfram
hugsaði um það eitt að komast áfram

bar hratt yfir

fylgdarmennirnir móðir og sveittir
en hún hafði engin orð
hraðaði sér í bæinn
til að hjálpa

það var mannúðar- og hetjulundin
hetjulund konu á torsóttri leið

wanted to keep on
wanted to continue
wanted to hear nothing mentioned but keeping on
thought only of continuing

carried swiftly forth

guidemen winded and sweaty
but she without a word
hurried into the house
to help

it was benevolence and heroism
the heroics of a woman on a trying path

~

Fæðingarstaðir þjóðarinnar
í fátæklegum fiskimannakofum
í hrörlegum baðstofum til sveita
í bátskeljum úti á sjó
í fjörugrjóti við óbyggðar heiðar
á grónum bölum í túnum

Birthplaces of the nation
in scant fishermen's huts
in decrepit country turfrooms
in toy rowboats out at sea
on rocky beaches by desolate heaths
on green grass banks in the fields

harðindi lágu í landi
allsleysi á allar hliðar
þó að eljað væri nótt með degi

aldrei neinn tími til
nema sá einn
sem fylltur var erli og önn og áhyggjum

allt kostaði áræði og manndóm
fásinna og einangrun og fátækt
setti svip á menn og híbýli þeirra

hardship ran rampant
destitution on all sides
despite striving night and day to survive

never any spare time
only the one
filled with toil and drudge and worry

everything cost daring and manpower
ignorance and isolation and poverty
characterized men and their dwellings

reykur og ryk engin þægindi til neins enginn ofn eða
tæki til upphitunar engin upphitun engin upphitun engar
olíuvélar né prímusar engin steinolíuvél eða prímus engin
hitunartæki engin eldstó nema hlóðirnar eldsneytið af
skornum skammti hálfrokkið inni loftræsting sama og
engin

þiljur gólf og loft
gliðnað í sundur
af elli og sliti
andrúmsloftið mettað raka og sagga
pollar á gólfum
lækur í göngunum

einn lítill olíulampi
grútartýra
vesæl grútartýra
kertisskar

eldurinn dauður

smoke and dust no comfort in anything no oven or device
for heat no heat no heat no oil machine or primus no
kerosene stove or primus no heater no furnace just an
open hearth fuel scarce halflit home ventilation same as
none

floor and ceiling panels
falling apart
from age and wear
air saturated with damp and must
puddles on the floors
streams in the walkway

one small oil lamp
blubberglow
meager codoilglow
candlestub

the fire dead

glugginn kafloðinn af hélu
gluggakistan einnig
gaddfreðið á glasinu sem konan átti að drekka úr
lá nærri að sængin væri frosin föst við vegginn
ekki til teskeið til að gefa barninu með
ekkert til nema frosinn hafragrautur

hvar átti að hita vatn?
hvar átti að þurrka fatnaðinn á barnið og konuna?

the window shaggy with hoarfrost
the windowledge as well
frozensolid the glass the woman was to drink from
the bedding near froze fast to the wall
not a teaspoon to feed the baby
nothing but frozen oatmeal

where was water to be heated?
where to dry clothes for the baby and woman?

eftir henni beðið
í innilegu trausti

öll ábyrgð á henni einni
að ráða fram úr hverjum vanda

með tvö stundum þrjú mannslíf í höndunum

for her they waited
in earnest trust

all responsibility on her alone
to overcome every problem

with two sometimes three lives in hand

sá hún ráð
þar sem aðrir reyndust ráðþrota
svo glögg á alla sjúkdómsgreiningu
örugg viss og æðrulaus
er vanda bar að höndum
hún vakti þegar aðrir sváfu

bar mótlæti með dæmafárri stillingu
bar mótlæti sem hetja
lét aldrei bugast

stillinguna þraut ekki
kjarkinn brast ekki
æðraðist ekki
á hverju sem gekk
óttalaus
á hverju sem gekk
hversu illa sem horfði
lét aldrei bugast

óbilandi

haggaðist ekki

she gave counsel
where others were confounded
so discerning about the whole diagnosis
trusty sure and dauntless
when trouble was at hand
she woke when others slept

bore adversity with unparalleled poise
bore adversity as a hero
never gave up

the poise unperturbed
the courage unbroken
despaired not
whatever came about
fearless
whatever came about
no matter how bad it looked
never gave up

unwavering

budged not

þar sem erfiðleikar voru mestir og fátt til úrræða
tók hún stjórnina í sínar hendur

þótti þá úr öllu rætast og allt verða greiðara
þar sem áður sýndust engar leiðir færar

where difficulties were greatest and resources few
she took command into her own hands

then all seemed to resolve and everything became easier
where before appeared no possible way

hvað konurnar glöddust
þegar hún kom til þeirra
um langan og erfiðan veg

engin kona sem fæddi barn vildi án hennar vera
lagni hennar og handtök rómuðu þær allar
rómuðu lipurð hennar og góðvild
dáðust að læknisviti hennar og snarræði
fundu hjá henni styrk og huggun

návist hennar jók þeim þrek í þrautum
vakti vonir og traust
hvarf allur ótti og kvíði
kvíði og hræðsla þvarr
jafnvel þjáningarnar minnkuðu

öll mein þóttu bætt
sem allar þrautir væru horfnar
sem allir erfiðleikar væru úr vegi ruddir
þá var öllu borgið
þegar hún var komin

how glad the women were
when she came to them
over the long and difficult road

no woman who birthed a child wanted to be without her
her deftness and touch were praised by all
praised her complaisance and goodwill
admired her healersense and vigilance
found strength and solace in her

her presence buttressed their spirit through struggle
sparked hope and confidence
dispelled all fear and anxiety
anxiety and fright dwindled
even agonies diminished

all harm felt mended
as all woes were vanished
as all difficulties were cleared away
then all was saved
when she had arrived

hún bar ljósið með sér
öryggi og yl
henni fylgdi
birtan og hlýjan

hún var sem Guðs engill
þegar mest á reið
vinur og verndari
vinur og ráðgjafi
í vanda og nauðum
verndarengill

sem öllum örðugleikum og vonleysi
væri vísað á dyr
þar sem hún var fyrir

allt varð gott
þegar hún var komin

nú kvíði ég engu
fyrst þú ert komin

she bore the light with her
safety and warmth
followed her
the brightness and the warmth

she was like God's angel
when most needed
friend and guardian
friend and counselor
in trouble and plight
guardian angel

all predicaments and hopelessness
were shown the door
when she was there

all was good
when she arrived

now I have no angst
since you have arrived

hún minnti á lindina tæru
sem vökvaði ungan gróður
gaf þyrstum og þjáðum svalandi drykk

þegar okkur reið mest á

she called to mind a clear spring
that watered new growth
gave the parched and pained slaking drink

when we were most in need

Þegar hún var að lauga barnið
kom sólin upp yfir fjallsbrúnina
og sveipaði barnið í kjöltu hennar sínum björtu geislum

dýrlegri sólarupprás hafði hún aldrei á ævi sinni séð

When she was bathing the baby
the sun came up over the mountainside
and wrapped bright rays round the babe in her lap

a more glorious sunrise she had never seen in her life

gleðin
hamingjan
einlæg djúp og heit

þegar fram úr rættist
þegar lífsneistinn glæddist

þá skein ljós
gleði og þakklætis
        hinu stærra og meira

ógleymanlegur fögnuður
undursamlegur friður
hátíðleg kyrrð
heilög gleði

fögnuðu hjörtu
nýjum vini
sem lífið hafði gefið þeim
að annast og unna

the joy
the happiness
sincere deep and fervent

when all worked out
when the lifespark flared

then shone the light
of joy and thanks
            for the higher and more

unforgettable elation
wonderful peace
solemn stillness
holy joy

rejoicing hearts
new friend
that life had given them
to care for and cherish

næturvakan hafði sínar fögru hliðar

yndisstundir

marga vornóttina horfði hún út um gluggann
meðan aðrir sváfu
með hugann svo opinn og næman
fyrir fegurð náttúrunnar og lífsins

útsýnið fagurt fjöllin blá
friður á starfsins brautum

starfsins sem gat ekki annað en hrært
við öllu því hlýjasta og besta
í konuhjarta

the nights awake had their beautiful sides

                              sweetwhiles

many spring nights she looked out the window
while others slept
with a mind so open and attuned
to the beauty of nature and life

the beautiful blue mountain view
peace in this work path

a job that could not help but stir
all the warmest and best
in womanheart

~

~

Hvað var henni svo goldið fyrir starf sitt og strit
ferðalög og fórnfýsi
lífshættur og vökunætur
vosbúð og þreytu?

What then was her compense for her task and toil
voyages and selfsacrifice
lifethreatening and wakeful nights
exposure and exhaustion?

fáar konur hafa utan heimilis unnið
jafn mikil erfið og vandasöm störf
fyrir jafn lítil laun

fyrir alla þessa hjálp tók hún sama sem enga borgun
marga ferðina fór hún fyrir ekki neitt
fór með guðsblessunina eina
gleði þess að hjálpa
líkna og hugga

þeim auði fær hvorki mölur né ryð grandað
eigi verður það með tölum talið né á vog vegið

few women have worked outside the home
at such difficult and demanding tasks
for as little

for all this help she took the same as no payment
many trips she made for nothing
went on godblessyous alone
this joy to help
nurse and console

neither moth nor rust can corrupt this wealth
it will not be tallied with numbers nor on scales weighed

hjartans þakklæti skrautritað ávarp í ramma veglegt samsæti skrautritað ávarp undirritað af konum margar veglegar gjafir vönduð heiðursgjöf bók með skrautrituðu ávarpi ávarp fégjafir og vinahót undirskriftir kvenna höfðingleg gjöf vönduð klukka fallegur steinhringur þakkarávarp árnaðaróskir vegleg veisla gjafir þakkar- og árnaðarorð veglegt samsæti veglegt samsæti vandað úr þakklæti og vinarhugur mörg þakklætisorð heiðurssamsæti minningargjöf saumakassi úr vönduðum viði með áletruðu nafni hennar ástúðarvottur vinafundur veglegt samsæti vandaður hægindastóll úr og klukka tryggð og vinarhugur vegleg skírnarskál úr silfri gjafir og þakkarávarp vandaður stóll peningagjöf veglegt samsæti kvæði fagrar gjafir skrautritað ljóð traust og virðing samsæti góðar gjafir vegleg veisla ræður ljóð minningargjöf samsæti vinsamleg ávörp minningargjafir þakklæti og vinarþel skrautritað ávarp búnaður á upphlut og næla vandaðir hlutir einlægur vinahugur hlýhugur og virðing samsæti í heiðurs- og þakklætisskyni vandaður gullhringur kvæði skrautritað ávarp og gullarmband góður reiðhestur vinsemd þakklæti og heiður kvæði vandað gullúr fjölmennt samsæti almennur hlýhugur

heartfelt gratitude a calligraphic letter in a frame splendid
gettogethers with coffee and cakes an address signed by
many women many splendid gifts a fine tribute book with
elegantly written dedications speech gifts of money and
expressions of friendship women's signatures noble gifts
fine clock a ring with a beautiful stone wellwishing thank
you speech splendid celebration gifts words of thanks and
goodwishes splendid gettogether a splendid gettogether a
fine watch gratitude and friendliness many gratefulwords
coffee and cake in her honor commemorativegift
sewingbox made of quality wood with her name inscribed
affectiontoken friendlygathering splendid gettogether
quality armchair watch and clock loyalty and friendship
a splendid silver baptismbasin gifts and thank you
speech a quality chair monetary gift splendid coffee and
cakes verses beautiful gifts calligraphic poetry trust and
respect gettogethers good gifts splendid celebration a
toast poetry commemorativegift coffee and cake friendly
speeches commemorativegifts gratitude and congeniality
elaborate speech precious metal upphlutur bodice ties belt
and brooch fine objects sincere friendship affection and
respect gettogethers in gratitude and honor a fine goldring

stórgjafir traust hlý vinátta og einlægt þakklæti samsæti
dýrar og vandaðar gjafir samsæti veglegt samsæti þakklæti
þakkarávarp rafmagnslampi gjörður af listamanni vinátta
og þakkarhugur samsæti veglegar gjafir skrautritað ljóð
gullúr með festi frá þakklátum konum fölskvalaus hlýhugur
kveðja og gjöf skjal með fallega orðaðri kveðju frá konum

verse elaborate speech goldbracelet good ridinghorse friendliness thanks honor and verse fine goldwatch a well attended gettogether general affection grand gifts trust warm friendship and sincere gratitude coffee and cake expensive fine gifts coffee cake splendid coffee and cakes thankfulness thank you speech an electric lamp made by an artist friendliness and thanks gettogethers with coffee and cake splendid gifts calligraphic poetry goldwatch and chain from grateful women unfeigned affection regards and gifts paper with beautifully worded regards from women

sjúkar vorum við
og þú vitjaðir okkar
styrk og róleg hefur þú staðið við hlið okkar
á erfiðum stundum
með góðleik þínum og gáfum
tekið innilegan þátt í gleði okkar
að afstaðinni þraut
sem þekking þín og gifta
leiddi ávallt til sigurs

we were sick
and you visited us
strong and calm you have stood by our side
in difficult moments
with your kindness and intelligence
took intimate part in our joy
that succeeded trial
as your knowledge and gifts
led invariably to victory

Ævikvöld hennar var kyrrlátt og milt
rökkrið færðist yfir smátt og smátt
það var eins og hún væri komin út fyrir tímann
og hann væri ekki til

við og við vaknaði hún til meðvitundar
líkt og þegar logi á útbrunnu skari blossar upp
þó að sjálft kertið sé brunnið niður í ljósastikuna

líf hennar og ævistarf var jafnan við það miðað
að vera viðbúin
þegar kallað var

og eins var nú
er síðasta kallið kom

Her twilight was quiet and mild
dusk moved over little by little
it was as if she had gone outside of time
                              and it did not exist

now and then she woke to consciousness
like when a flame on a burntout wick flares up
though the candle itself has burned down to the base

her life and lifework were based on constance
on being ready
when called

and so she was now
when the last call came

áratug eftir áratug flýtti hún sér til starfa
hins daglega lífs
var aldrei frá verki

eins og reyndur formaður og sigurhetja
leit hún yfir farinn veg

allt líf hennar var henni lof

decade after decade she hurried to the job
her daily life
was never away from work

as an experienced captain and winninghero
she looked back on the journey made

her entire life attested to her character

hennar var sárt saknað
þegar hún var kölluð heim
til landsins ókunna
hvarf yfir hafið
hvarf yfir landamærin miklu

she was sorely missed
when she was called home
to the land unknown
gone over the sea
gone over the great divide

sál hennar lifir hjá Guði
en verk hennar áhrif og menning
hjá mönnunum

konunnar með heita hjartað sem bræddi ís og snjó
konunnar með stálviljann sem hastaði á vind og vötn
var ævinlega komin þar sem þörfin var mest

her soul lives with God
but her work influence and culture
among men

the woman with the hot heart that melted ice and snow
the woman with the steelwill that soothed wind and water
was found forever where the need was most

kistan sveipuð svörtum flauelsfeldi
og engir blómsveigar skreyttu hana

kærleiksminningin
er dýrlegasti kransinn
á hinni blómlausu kistu

the coffin wrapped in black velvet
and no adorning floral garlands

lovingmemory
the most glorious wreath
on the flowerless coffin

THE MIDWIVES
LJÓSMÆÐURNAR

Þorbjörg Sveinsdóttir

Þórunn Ástríður
  Björnsdóttir

Guðrún Gísladóttir

Guðrún J. Norðfjörð

Guðfríður Jóhannesdóttir

Matthildur Þorkelsdóttir

Björg Magnúsdóttir

Hákonía Jóhanna
  Hákonardóttir

Kristín Jónsdóttir

Þuríður Guðmundsdóttir

Sigríður K. Jónsdóttir

Ingibjörg Jósepsdóttir

Margrét Jónsdóttir

Petrea Guðný Gísladóttir

Hallbera Jónsdóttir

Helga Indriðadóttir

Pálína Guðný Björnsdóttir

Jakobína Sveinsdóttir

Þórunn Hjörleifsdóttir

Sigurfljóð Einarsdóttir

Björg Hjörleifsdóttir

Guðrún Jónína Stefánsdóttir

Þórunn Gísladóttir

Margrét Gísladóttir

Þórdís Símonardóttir

Sigríður Eiríksdóttir Sæland

Sólveig Pálsdóttir

Guðbjörg Hannesdóttir

Ásgerður Gunnlaugsdóttir

Ingveldur Pétursdóttir

Þórunn Magnúsdóttir

Pálína Sveinsdóttir

Emilía Biering

Guðný Þórarinsdóttir

Elín Jónsdóttir
Magðalena Guðlaugsdóttir
Ingibjörg Jónasdóttir
Ólína Sigurðardóttir
Margrét Grímsdóttir
Ólína Sveinsdóttir
María Hafliðadóttir
Rósa Jónsdóttir Thorlacius
Sigurlína Einarsdóttir
Ágústína Gunnarsdóttir
Sigurbjörg Jónsdóttir
Rannveig Jónsdóttir
Guðrún Halldórsdóttir
Aðalbjörg Pálsdóttir
Kristrún Bóasdóttir
Guðlaug H. Þorgrímsdóttir
Ragnhildur Jónsdóttir
Arndís Eiríksdóttir
Anna Valgerður
    Benediktsdóttir
Ingibjörg Þórðardóttir
Margrét Jónsdóttir
Jóhanna Friðriksdóttir
Jórunn Jónsdóttir

Björg Pétursdóttir
Þórunn Jónsdóttir
Guðríður Eiríksdóttir
Sigríður Jónsdóttir
Hjálmfríður Lilja
    Bergsveinsdóttir
Ragnheiður I. Jónsdóttir
Sólveig Guðmundsdóttir
Matthildur Grímsdóttir
Guðrún Jónsdóttir
Halldóra Jóhannsdóttir
Ingibjörg Frímannsdóttir
Hólmfríður Friðfinnsdóttir
Albína S. Bergsdóttir
Oddný Baldvinsdóttir
Þorbjörg Sigurhjartardóttir
Katrín Sveinsdóttir
Anna Kristín Sigurðardóttir
Friðrika Jónsdóttir
Margrét Richardsdóttir
Sigrún Sigurjónsdóttir
Hallfríður Brandsdóttir
Björg Jónsdóttir
Þórunn Pálsdóttir

Guðrún Sigurðardóttir
Katrín Sigurðardóttir
Sigríður Pálsdóttir
Kristín Eiríksdóttir
Guðrún Þorláksdóttir
Halldóra Þorsteinsdóttir
Sigríður Ísleifsdóttir
Ljótunn Þorsteinsdóttir
Guðrún Pálsdóttir
Ingunn Stefánsdóttir
Guðrún Aradóttir
Lydía Pálsdóttir
Hildur Jónsdóttir
Matthildur Guðmundsdóttir
Þorbjörg Jónsdóttir
Þórunn Jónsdóttir
Sigurlaug Vigfúsdóttir
Elísabet Þorsteinsdóttir
Guðrún Einarsdóttir
Jórunn Guðmundsdóttir

Historical Background

Sögulegt samhengi

At the end of the nineteenth century, Iceland was a poor and thinly populated country with around 70,000 residents. The vast majority were farmers in the countryside. Towns were few and small. The highlands in the center of the country are uninhabitable, so Icelanders lived—and still live—closer to the coast. Transportation was difficult, as the island's position in the middle of the North Atlantic creates volatile weather conditions and long, dark winters. There were almost no roads nor bridges but plenty of dangerous mountains to pass, rivers, lava fields, etc. People travelled by foot or on horseback, following cairns on common routes. The south coast was especially challenging, because of the great sands and glacial rivers—the ring road around Iceland wasn't finished until 1974, when the last rivers on the south coast were bridged. Today, most Icelanders live in urban areas, the majority around the capital, but most of the midwives in this book lived and worked in the old farming communities of rural Iceland.

The first educated midwives, as well as the first doctors, were officially appointed in Iceland in the late eighteenth century. Midwifery was the first profession open to women. Doctors were few and far between, so there were a lot of people without formal education practising folk medicine all over the island, among them midwives who were sometimes said to be both the ljósmóðir (midwife) and the læknir (doctor) of their county. Midwifery was a demanding job, since the midwife had to be ready to leave her home night or day, in summer or winter, and embark on an often long and difficult journey to a labouring woman. Most people were poor farmers and conditions at home were frequently bad. Infant mortality was very high in Iceland, not least because most Icelandic women gave their babies cow milk instead of breastfeeding them, but it started to decrease in the late nineteenth century, with better education of midwives, improved hygiene, and health professionals' promotion of breastfeeding.

For centuries, almost all women in Iceland gave birth at home. This changed around the middle of the twentieth century when women increasingly started giving birth in hospitals. Midwives have, however, always been the main providers of maternal care, be it in or outside a hospital, and a doctor only steps in if something goes wrong. The move into hospitals was later criticized as a medicalization of pregnancy and birth; in the last decades there has been a new emphasis on the mother's choice and various alternative possibilities to the typical hospital environment. Midwives have spearheaded this initiative, successfully working to ensure diverse birthing practices are supported by Iceland's centralized state welfare system, which is funded by taxes and provides everybody with health care, including maternal care before, during and after birth.

Kristín Svava Tómasdóttir

Author & Translator Conversation
Höfundur og þýðandi spjalla saman

K. B. Thors: How about we start with the story of how you decided to put this book together?

Kristín Svava Tómasdóttir: Yes! I've always liked working with found material in my poetry, and I'd had it at the back of my mind to do something a bit bigger and more systematic in that vein. Then, for a separate historical research project, I picked up a book I'd read a few years before and been absolutely fascinated by—or books, there are three volumes—called *Íslenskar ljósmæður*, *Icelandic Midwives*, containing short biographical entries about midwives working in Iceland in earlier times. Compiled by two priests and published by one of them, Rev. Sveinn Víkingur, they describe the women's upbringing and how they became midwives, their experiences, and their lives' work. Some entries are written by the midwives

themselves, others by old friends, descendants or some-
one else who knew them or knew of them, and a few texts
are written by Rev. Sveinn Víkingur himself. Most of the
midwives included were working in the nineteenth or
early twentieth century, maybe a handful as early as the
late eighteenth century.

Most of these midwives were working in rural Iceland
and stories about their difficult travels are an important
part of the text, describing, often quite dramatically, how
they had to leave their homes in the middle of the night and
travel through all sorts of winter weather and treacherous
terrain to help women get through labour. Women were, in
general, much more confined to the home than the men, so
the midwives' position was in that sense unique.

I would classify these midwife stories as part of a
beloved Icelandic literary genre, "þjóðlegur fróðleikur"—
it's a kind of folk history or local lore in print, where dan-
gerous and often deadly travels in the Icelandic wilderness
in earlier times are a significant theme. I love "þjóðlegur
fróðleikur", both the blind and chaotic passion for accu-
mulating local historical knowledge and the storytelling
itself—but it is quite male-dominated, especially the travel
stories. I'm only half-joking when I say that there are more
sheep and horses named in those stories than women
(there are whole books on the lives and personalities of

distinctive sheep and horses, as described by their owners). Because of this, the stories in *Icelandic Midwives* are so unique and lovely; these are rare stories of women who courageously took on harrowing and dangerous travels, to perform acts of kindness and support. Most lived to tell about it, but two of the midwives included died while on the job. Margrét Richardsdóttir was killed in an avalanche when crossing a steep scarp in the east of Iceland in 1895, Helga Indriðadóttir drowned in a river in the north in 1905. The two poems of the book beginning with "the fey will not be saved", "ekki verður feigum forðað", draw on the stories of their deaths—that phrase is used in both narratives.

As I read *Icelandic Midwives* more closely, I started noticing certain narrative themes and motifs in the stories which I found intriguing. The fatalistic repetition of "the fey will not be saved" is one example. Many authors emphasized that this or that midwife had served *the* most difficult district in Iceland. Obviously, that could not be strictly true for all of them. Many authors also wrote that neither a baby nor a mother had ever died in the hands of a particular midwife. This is also not very credible, based on the high mortality of both babies and women in labour at the time. I was fascinated by the similarities in the construction of the narratives and the descriptions of the midwives' virtues and their work. That is when I had the idea of working with these texts, using them as raw material for poetry. I love repetitions in poetry, to create rhythm and emphasize meaning, and I wondered if I could use the thematic and linguistic repetitions in the texts to create repetitions and rhythm in the poems.

I was a bit hesitant to delve into it, because it was such a lot of handiwork and I wasn't certain if it was going to work, but when Covid hit and I started spending a lot of time at home in the spring of 2020, I decided to just get on with it and see how it would come out. I went through *Icelandic Midwives*, taking extensive notes of what I thought I could use. Then I went through the notes a few times, trimming them a bit each time. The text I ended up with I then sorted thematically into chapters: childhood and calling, travel and weather, etc. When the structure of the work was there, I started actually making it into poetry, arranging and rearranging words and phrases— all the text, every word, is taken from *Icelandic Midwives*, but I've cut and pasted freely and I did sometimes change the grammatical cases, plural to singular or vice versa, to make it fit better together.

KBT: In 2013 Icelanders held a vote on the Icelandic language, looking for fegursta orðið—the most beautiful word. Ljósmóðir won. The working title for this book was *Fegursta orðið*. How did it become *Hetjusögur*?

KST: The word ljósmóðir literally means mother of light; it is composed of two words which are both already heavy with meaning, ljós = light and móðir = mother. My twofold objective with the book was to a) spotlight these amazing stories of women of the past, to help them take their rightful place in history, and b) use poetry to take apart the narratives themselves, to look at how the stories about these women had been told, what kind of language was used and what was thought worthy to say and play up. Referencing the romanticized status of the word ljósmóðir itself would have been fitting in a way, but there is a book by another Icelandic poet, Linda Vilhjálmsdóttir, called *Öll fallegu orðin, All the Beautiful Words*, which I thought might be slightly too similar. In the end, I was really happy with *Hetjusögur, Herostories*, because like the work itself, it can be read both in-your-face literally, with an emphasis on the heroes, and alternatively and more critically with an emphasis on the stories. The English version then wonderfully adds another layer, where you can skip the o: *Her(o)stories*. As a historian, I've specialized partly in women's and gender history so this history/herstory wordplay is very familiar.

It should be mentioned that in earlier times, there was another word more commonly used in Icelandic for midwife, yfirsetukona, a woman that "sits over" or "sits by" a woman in labour—more descriptive but much less romantic. Ljósmóðir gained hold in the twentieth century, probably because people thought it sounded nicer!

KBT: Comparing "lightmother" to "midwife" did give me mixed feelings! Though midwife is similar to yfirsetu- kona—deriving from the Old English mid, "with", and wif, "woman". There's one place in the translation where I inserted a line. The poem "strong but still soft and mild" ends with "lightmotherhands" and then an additional "midwifehands". It felt important to have the light and mother present—this is the only instance of that direct translation in the English. Fortunately your repetition made doubling that final word quite natural, so we have the familiar meaning resounding too.

The Icelandic word "saga" means both history and story. There are two "sagas" in the book's second poem, lay- ering that meaning. Do you feel like this project was a nat- ural extension of your previous work as a poet-historian, or more of a branching out?

KST: Initially, I didn't really think about my poetry and

my historical writing as much connected. I was a poet before I started studying history—I published my first book in my first semester at university, after a few years participating in readings and publishing in magazines—and I was always very grateful for having that identity unrelated to the academic world. I felt it made me less dependent on following in the conventional academic footsteps, and I liked keeping it separate.

But in the last years, I've seen more and more similarities between what I'm writing as a poet and as a historian. As a historian, you're working primarily with language and text, picking its meaning apart, being suspicious of people's conscious and unconscious intentions, and then when you start writing you also must be critical of your own language and aware of all the nuances and subtleties in meaning. I wrote my MA thesis, and then a monograph, on the history of the concept of pornography in Iceland, and I think that affected my thoughts on language a lot. The topic is fraught with unspoken beliefs and moral judgments and it's so clear in those discussions how people use certain words, phrases and clichés to express their outlook and their taste and so to assert their identity. I think there's a certain growing suspiciousness that comes through in my poetry towards language and how it is used.

Herostories is a fuller and more intentional bringing

together than before of my work as a poet and as a historian but it is poetry, not history. The way I see it, I'm using the tools of poetry to tackle historical material which I would usually write about in a different way. I was very happy that it ended up being published in 2020, at the same time as another book that I participated in writing, *Konur sem kjósa*, which is a history of women as political agents in Iceland from 1915—when Icelandic women won the vote—up to our days and is also a project which partly aims to bring women into mainstream national history. It was nice to have them side by side, very different but still connected in a meaningful way.

When you told me you had begun translating the book, my first thought was that you had lost your mind! It seemed such a crazy task, because of how the text is composed. When I read and commented on your translation of *Stormwarning*, I would refer to how something came out compared to the original, meaning the Icelandic version, but it is more difficult to use the concept of "the original" in the case of *Herostories*. The working material are texts written around the middle of the twentieth century, telling stories that mostly took place 50–100 years before, but the final version is a poetry book from the twenty-first century, so in a way you're working with two or three layers of language and tone. Reading it over, I would for example sometimes wonder if a certain word felt too modern—but it is a modern book after all! How was it for you as a translator to navigate this?

KBT: Pretty wild! After *Stormwarning* I was almost certain I'd translate your next book of poems. Then you explained how this new book was about historical midwives. Then I read *Hetjusögur* and my mind was blown because not only were you telling these midwives' stories, you were messing with this multilayered critique of gendered labor and narrative! I *had* to translate it.

I didn't want to stray too far from your source texts, words these women and people closer to them in time used. I tried to keep things simple and quite direct, but then sometimes read over and felt the poem just wasn't there. Knowing it was found text made me a timid translator, but that dissatisfaction helped me lose that timidity over time. One of the first poems I translated uses the word "sheriff". That came after I gave myself a little shake and tried to tune into not what the poem said, but how it felt. When I first sent that to you, I was bracing to explain myself! Alternatives like "county manager" or "district boss" seemed so stiff.

I learned a lot about history and etymology, checking on when and how words came into use. Looking terms up led me to old news articles, meteorology reports, church birth and baptism records, etc., which helped me connect with different time periods. Sometimes I'd imagine someone writing a letter at an old desk around 1900. That became a mood test.

It was late 2020 when I started translating this, deep in Montreal's winter. Being able to gear up and head to "the mountain"—enough forest to get lost in, layered in snow—was a godsend. After reading about avalanches and blankets frozen to the wall, I'd come back and marvel at hot running water! I was grateful for this project during that time. My aunt Ellen was a huge help. She patiently answered many hair-splitting questions, and her big old Icelandic-English dictionaries outdid mine and the internet more than once.

It took me a while to grasp how you were really going *in* on how we talk about and praise these women and their work! And I was still sort of shocked, between being amazed by the midwives. How did it feel to critique such a precious topic? I found it exhilarating to feel such holy ground be fair game. It really showed how pedestals for emotional service are not helping!

KST: I think the ambiguity was the key, the fact that this is both praise *and* critique. I felt secure and sincere in my appreciation of these women and the books written about them, so I didn't feel bad about tearing at the romanticized female image that is undoubtedly there—the woman and the image are not the same, after all, or the woman and the narrative. My experience as a historian probably helped me with this since it's often such an integral part of writing history to try and combine empathy with pointed critical analysis.

The material is so rich when it comes to how these ideal women are described. Early in the translation process, for example, we had a long discussion about the word "vanity". In the chapter about the longing for education and broader horizons, there is a poem that describes the reasons for a woman wanting to become a midwife: "out of / childishness and curiosity / curiosity and vanity". Vanity is a direct translation of the Icelandic hégómaskapur but it suddenly struck me when reading over the translation—why on earth would you call wanting to be a midwife vanity? Isn't this job, after all, supposed to be the epitome of selflessness? I looked the original up in *Icelandic Midwives* and found that I had taken the words from a woman who describes her great admiration for a midwife that she knew when she was a girl, and how her decision to become a midwife herself might be explained by "the vanity of wanting to be like this woman". I still found it a curious choice of words, and maybe it reveals how impossible it was for her and others to conform to the ideal of what a woman should want to be—even if you're choosing this remarkable and highly regarded caring profession, the fact that there might be something of your own desire there, of wanting to do something different than other women, arouses suspicion. We discussed if there was a possibility of using another word in this poem, with less negative connotations, but in the end, this was the direct translation of how a midwife told her own story.

KBT: Reading *Hetjusögur*, the timing was amazing because I had just learned that my Amma, my Icelandic grandmother, used to say "allt er hégómi". "All is vanity". So crossing paths with this page gave me a shiver. Getting startled like that was a good chance to get more into context. This poem reminded me of how, like many women in these poems, my Amma was a spiritual lady. Synonyms for vanity include pride, self-love, and self-esteem, but that's not what the poem said.

Iceland is known as a book-loving nation with a literary tradition heavy on reading in the home. It's at or near the top of lists ranking "best countries for women". But these poems frame "girls learning to write!" as outlandish.

Who would Petrea Guðný Gísladóttir have been hiding her learning from?

KST: Hiding their attempts at writing, practising in secret, is something you find in many narratives from women who grew up in the nineteenth century, among them Petrea Guðný who is one of my favourite mid-wives in the book. She was from a poor rural family in the west of Iceland but had a great desire for educa-tion and managed to move to Reykjavík in the 1880s, when she was in her late twenties, where she studied Danish, cooking, and eventually midwifery. She woke up at four in the morning to study, worked from six AM to two PM to be able to afford her education and then went to classes. Today Icelandic gender equality is, like the literary tradition, part of a certain national image that is played up, but that is a relatively recent phenomenon. From the mid-eighteenth century, both girls and boys were supposed to learn to read, but the emphasis on writ-ing came later and many considered it useless for girls to learn to write—and sometimes called it vanity. Everybody had to be able to read religious texts, but it was another thing to put your own words on paper.

KBT: The poem "out of" lists compulsions toward midwifery. How might an elfwoman's promise have gotten a girl into this line of work?

KST: There used to be a strong belief in elves in Iceland, or "hidden people", invisible people who lived in hills and rocks. Sometimes they made themselves visible to humans and even sought help from them, for example when an elfwoman was in labour and needed a woman to sit with her. (You might read in promotional material for tourists that many Icelanders still believe in hidden people. I think that's more performance than reality, but that's another story.) The hidden people are mentioned in some of the midwives' stories. The elfwoman's promise is taken from the story of a midwife in the Westfjords, who met an elfwoman when she was young and helped her give birth. The elfwoman in turn promised that she would always have fortune in this kind of work and the woman eventually became a successful midwife.

KBT: There's so much weather in this book. The first "fey will not be saved" taught me that "krap", which I'd translated as "slush" might also be snow mixed with seawater. As you put it in our notes, "they would´ve gone down the canyon under the snow and then the avalanche continues in the water and carries them to sea". This ocean avalanche, and then the land described over and over as ófærð, un-goable or impassable. It was hard not to theorize about weather norms when all it takes to change "going" to "ungoable" is an ó, and ófærð is everywhere. "Impassable" isn't very frequently used in English conversation, but it still felt like the best fit.

KST: Ófærð is such a common word in Icelandic, I had never thought about it like that before. Well-travelled roads regularly become impassable in the wintertime and have to be closed, sometimes for days. Nature has her say, and you are stuck—*Ófærð* is actually the original title for the Icelandic crime series *Trapped* which aired internationally a few years ago. This was even more significant in the old days, when there were no mountain trucks and people had to go on horseback or "on apostles' horses" like it says in one of the poems—on foot.

It seems I'm getting more obsessed with the weather myself with each book, the last one obviously being called *Stormwarning*. The dramatic weather descriptions were definitely one of the reasons I became so infatuated with *Icelandic Midwives*. I had the idea early on to use the weather words and phrases to make imposing blocks of text that sound breathless or almost suffocating when you read them out loud. They were one of the reasons I worried about your sanity when translating the book!

KBT: Those blocks were real slogs. I kept feeling they weren't quite vivid enough. Eventually I cut and pasted the word "rok" a bit freely, like you made the original poems—that's the only word I did that with in the book. It's so sharp and efficient, it felt natural to carry the drama into the translation. Adding a couple instances and using it as a synonym helped achieve both rhythm and the formal wall of text. Many Anglo readers are familiar with it and if not, the context is definitely there.

KST: Icelanders love to brag about how many words the language has for different kinds of weather, especially bad weather, wind and snow and so forth. Many of these words are compounds, which are common in Icelandic. The poem that begins with "and the river cannot be avoided", for example, has "stórfljót flóðmikil straumþung stórgrýtt", all majestic-sounding words but still very recognizable and normal compounds in Icelandic. They become "major-river greatflood heavycurrents bigboulders" in your translation. I hesitated at these unusual English compounds at first, wondering if they sounded too experimental and we had a discussion about it—it's always this treading of the line between staying true to the tone of the historical material but also to the nature of the book as a twenty-first century literary work. As I mentioned to you in our talks, I'm working with a certain defamiliarization in the Icelandic text as well, drawing attention to "old language" in a new context, in a way that's difficult to replicate in translation. How did you come to this technique and how did it develop through the translation process?

KBT: When *Hetjusögur* came out my aunt sent me a clip of you reading "Aldrei var skammdegismyrkrið" on Icelandic TV. That was another early poem I translated, and I felt strongly about "skammdegismyrkrið" becoming "the shortdaydark", basically the literal breakdown of the word (with a "ness" trimmed for sound). The darkness of short northern winter days is so central to Icelandic life there's a single, compound word for it; to divide that word into a phrase would undermine that centrality. Using words like "shortdaydark" and "poemscrap" also reflected the originals' stark appearance on the page, which to me spoke to your collage of source fragments. Compounds left readers space to puzzle out meanings, which I figured they would. Puzzling out is part of the experience of reading this book, peering into text.

Like you said, the weather descriptions are made with common Icelandic words. English vernacular can't compete with them, and I didn't want fanciful synonyms distancing us from intense storms. The weather poems get scarier as the layers pile on, and compounds allowed for more layers of immediately recognizable ingredients like "howling" and "blizzard". It helps that simpler compound moments precede the block poems, and the blocks are long enough that a reader could get used to what was happening. Rather than confusion, hopefully the effect is a feeling of being barraged and walled in by weather.

Compounds were also a way for me to emphasize excess when, say, the praise of a midwife's virtue is so effusive it becomes suspect. The big block praise poem is a key moment in the book. At first words like "conscientiousness" felt clunky, despite being appropriate for the time, but then they seemed to fit in the world of handiness, diligence, and bodilyendurance. Compounds and suffixes were a way to move the translation toward the excess of the original. Repetition in word structure—not something that comes as naturally in English as in less motley languages—intensified the list, all these -nesses. Your roasting style is often subtle, but the praise block was a place I could lean into this onslaught and give tonal clues that yes, this is getting absurd.

Religion is another recurring element in these poems. As we were exchanging notes on these translations, Roe v. Wade was overturned in the US. Can you touch on the relationship between church, state, and midwifery in Iceland? The poems speak to the spiritual sides of this labor.

KST: It was obvious from the beginning that I had to include a chapter on the midwives' relationship with God. Iceland was a religious society in the nineteenth century and there's both a religious outlook that comes through in these narratives and a certain fatalism, which I guess was natural in circumstances where you had limited chances to shape your own life and were often at the mercy of nature. The midwives of course drew on their own experience and knowledge but in the end, they put their faith in God; He worked through them.

The Lutheran church is still tied to the state in Iceland today, as a national church, which for me is truly one of the mysteries of Icelandic politics. It's almost like nobody can be bothered to sever the tie. Iceland is a very secular society and religious morals have little hold. Attitudes towards sex and relationships are rather casual, for example, and I would say that Icelanders in general are not very dogmatic. The church does not have a central place in public life. Most people only go to church for concerts or ceremonies like baptisms, weddings and funerals. I'm sure there are still midwives in Iceland that are religious but it's certainly not talked about in the same way as in earlier times.

I wonder how American readers will understand and react to these poems. I loved the American reviews of *Stormwarning*, the comments were so on point and more perceptive than many of the reviews I got in Iceland. (Sorry, Icelandic reviewers!) I realize there's a more complicated context with *Herostories*.

KBT: Yes, it's not just that Iceland's health care is centralized and tax funded. Where Iceland's midwives have always been within the evolving system, North American midwives were effectively gatekept from official modern health care. I'm also curious about how American audiences will react to the text. I think the poems can shed light on birthing practices while highlighting historic parallels between midwifery traditions in different cultural contexts. I don't know how sarcastic poems about a midwife's track record will land, given the current cultural climate, but I know how energizing and powerful this text was for me. I hope this translation allows others to feel something along those lines.

August 2022

Acknowledgments
Þakkir

Our appreciation goes out to the editors at *Northwest Review, Waxwing, Loch Raven Review,* and *Anomaly* for publishing excerpts of these translations.

Thank you all
for your support.
We do this for you,
and could not do
it without you.

PARTNERS

pixel █ texel

EMBREY FAMILY
FOUNDATION

★ ALLRED
CAPITAL MANAGEMENT
of
RAYMOND JAMES®

ADDITIONAL DONORS, CONT'D

Mike Soto
Mokhtar Ramadan
Nikki & Dennis Gibson
Patrick Kukucka
Patrick Kutcher
Rev. Elizabeth & Neil Moseley
Richard Meyer
Scott & Katy Nimmons
Sherry Perry

Sydneyann Binion
Stephen Harding
Stephen Williamson
Susan Carp
Susan Ernst
Theater Jones
Tim Perttula
Tony Thomson

SUBSCRIBERS

Caroline West
Elizabeth Simpson
Nicole Yurcaba
Jennifer Owen
Melanie Nicholls
Alan Glazer
Matt Bucher
Katarzyna Bartoszynska
Michael Binkley
Erin Kubatzky
Michael Lighty
Joseph Rebella
Jarratt Willis
Heustis Whiteside
Samuel Herrera
Josh Rubenoff
Reid Sharpless
Damon Copeland
Kyle Trimmer
Kenneth McClain
Scott Chiddister

Ryan Todd
Petra Hendrickson
Austin Dearborn
Hillary Richards
Nancy Keaton
Nancy Allen
John Mitchell
Sian Valvis
Jessica Sirs
Courtney Sheedy
John Andrew Margrave
John Tenny
Dauphin Ewart
Heath Dollar
Conner Cunningham
Tom Bowden
Margaret Terwey
Jona Gerlach
Sabrina Balgamwalla
Harriman
Whitney O Banner

Jeffrey Nichols
Hannah Good
Ashley Cline
Vee Kalkunte
Connor Shirley
Jack Waters
Stephen Fuller
Kirsten Murchison
Jennifer Caroll
Agi Bori Mottern
Margaret Cochran
Crystal Cardenas
Alina Stefanescu Coryell
Kate Sherrod
Angela Schlegel
Michael Peirson
Marya Hart
Carole Hailey

AVAILABLE NOW FROM DEEP VELLUM

MARIA GABRIELA LLANSOL • *The Geography of Rebels Trilogy: The Book of Communities; The Remaining Life; In the House of July & August* • translated by Audrey Young • PORTUGAL

TEDI LÓPEZ MILLS • *The Book of Explanations* • translated by Robin Myers • MEXICO

PABLO MARTÍN SÁNCHEZ • *The Anarchist Who Shared My Name* • translated by Jeff Diteman • SPAIN

DOROTA MASŁOWSKA • *Honey, I Killed the Cats* • translated by Benjamin Paloff • POLAND

BRICE MATTHIEUSSENT • *Revenge of the Translator* • translated by Emma Ramadan • FRANCE

LINA MERUANE • *Seeing Red* • translated by Megan McDowell • CHILE

ANTONIO MORESCO • *Clandestinity* • translated by Richard Dixon • ITALY

VALÉRIE MRÉJEN • *Black Forest* • translated by Katie Shireen Assef • FRANCE

FISTON MWANZA MUJILA • *Tram 83* • translated by Roland Glasser • *The River in the Belly: Poems* • translated by J. Bret Maney • DEMOCRATIC REPUBLIC OF CONGO

GORAN PETROVIĆ • *At the Lucky Hand, aka The Sixty-Nine Drawers* • translated by Peter Agnone • SERBIA

LUDMILLA PETRUSHEVSKAYA • *The New Adventures of Helen: Magical Tales* • translated by Jane Bugaeva • RUSSIA

ILJA LEONARD PFEIJFFER • *La Superba* • translated by Michele Hutchison • NETHERLANDS

RICARDO PIGLIA • *Target in the Night* • translated by Sergio Waisman • ARGENTINA

SERGIO PITOL • *The Art of Flight* • *The Journey* • *The Magician of Vienna* • *Mephisto's Waltz: Selected Short Stories* • *The Love Parade* • translated by George Henson • MEXICO

JULIE POOLE • *Bright Specimen* • USA

EDUARDO RABASA • *A Zero-Sum Game* • translated by Christina MacSweeney • MEXICO

ZAHIA RAHMANI • *"Muslim": A Novel* • translated by Matt Reeck • FRANCE/ALGERIA

MANON STEFFAN ROS • *The Blue Book of Nebo* • WALES

JUAN RULFO • *The Golden Cockerel & Other Writings* • translated by Douglas J. Weatherford • MEXICO

IGNACIO RUIZ-PÉREZ • *Isles of Firm Ground* • translated by Mike Soto • MEXICO

ETHAN RUTHERFORD • *Farthest South & Other Stories* • USA

TATIANA RYCKMAN • *Ancestry of Objects* • USA

JIM SCHUTZE • *The Accommodation* • USA

OLEG SENTSOV • *Life Went On Anyway* • translated by Uilleam Blacker • UKRAINE

MIKHAIL SHISHKIN • *Calligraphy Lesson: The Collected Stories* • translated by Marian Schwartz, Leo Shtutin, Mariya Bashkatova, Sylvia Maizell • RUSSIA

ÓFEIGUR SIGURÐSSON • *Öræfi: The Wasteland* • translated by Lytton Smith • ICELAND

NOAH SIMBLIST, ed. • *Tania Bruguera: The Francis Effect* • CUBA

DANIEL SIMON, ed. • *Dispatches from the Republic of Letters* • USA

MUSTAFA STITOU • *Two Half Faces* • translated by David Colmer • NETHERLANDS

SOPHIA TERAZAWA • *Winter Phoenix: Testimonies in Verse* • USA

MÄRTA TIKKANEN • *The Love Story of the Century* • translated by Stina Katchadourian • SWEDEN

ROBERT TRAMMELL • *Jack Ruby & the Origins of the Avant-Garde in Dallas & Other Stories* • USA

BENJAMIN VILLEGAS • *ELPASO: A Punk Story* • translated by Jay Noden • SPAIN

S. YARBERRY • *A Boy in the City* • USA

SERHIY ZHADAN • *Voroshilovgrad* • translated by Reilly Costigan-Humes & Isaac Wheeler • UKRAINE

FORTHCOMING FROM DEEP VELLUM